Steve Jobs

www.pegasusforkids.com

© **B. Jain Publishers (P) Ltd.** All rights reserved. No part of this book may be reproduced, stored in a retrieval system or transmitted, in any form or by any means, mechanical, photocopying, recording or otherwise, without any prior written permission of the publisher.

Published by Kuldeep Jain for B. Jain Publishers (P) Ltd., D-157, Sector 63, Noida - 201307, U.P
Registered office: 1921/10, Chuna Mandi, Paharganj, New Delhi-110055

Printed in India

Contents

- 5   Who was Steve Jobs?
- 6   Birth and Early Years
- 9   Education and Career
- 16   The Beginning of Apple I
- 24   Early Days of Apple
- 30   Preparing for the Future
- 34   Macintosh
- 40   Steve Quits Apple
- 44   Beginning of NeXT
- 49   Personal Life
- 54   Jobs Returns to Apple
- 61   The End of a Super Inventor
- 64   Timeline
- 68   Activities
- 71   Glossary

Who was Steve Jobs?

Steven Paul Jobs was an American businessman. He is best known as the co-founder, chairman, and chief executive officer (CEO) of Apple Inc. He was the CEO and largest shareholder of Pixar Animation Studios; a member of The Walt Disney Company's board of directors following its acquisition of Pixar; and founder, chairman, and CEO of NeXT Inc. Jobs is widely acknowledged as a pioneer of the microcomputer revolution of the 1970s, along with Apple co-founder Steve Wozniak. Jobs is often described as the creative entrepreneur whose passion for perfection and ferocious drive revolutionized the six industries personal computers, animated movies, music, phones, tablet computing, and digital publishing.

Birth and Early Years

Steven Paul Jobs was born on February 24, 1955, in San Francisco, California to Abdulfattah 'John' Jandali and Joanne Schieble. Being born out of wedlock in the puritan America of the 1950s, Jobs was put up for adoption. His father, Jandali, was a Syrian political science professor, and his mother, Joanne, worked as a speech therapist. Shortly after Jobs was placed for adoption, his biological parents married and had another child, Mona Simpson. It was not until Jobs was 27 that he came to know of his biological parents.

Joanne had a college education, and she insisted that the future parents of her boy be just as well educated. Unfortunately, the candidates, Paul and Clara Jobs, who adopted the child, did not meet her expectations. Clara worked as an accountant while Paul was a Coast Guard and machinist. The family lived in Mountain View, California,

within the area that would later become known as Silicon Valley. Paul and Clara called their son Steven Paul. They adopted another baby, called Patti, three years later in 1958.

As a boy, Jobs and his father worked on electronic gadgets in the family garage. Paul showed his son how to take apart and reconstruct gadgets, a hobby that instilled confidence, tenacity and mechanical prowess in young Jobs.

Education and Career

Even though Jobs was always an intelligent and innovative thinker, his youth was marked by frustration over formal schooling. Jobs was a prankster in elementary school as he was bored, and his fourth-grade teacher— Imogene "Teddy" Hill—had to bribe him to study. She bribed him with candy and US$ 5 from her own money. Jobs became so hooked to this idea that he skipped the fifth grade and went straight to middle school—Crittenden Middle School. The school was located in a poor area. Most kids did not work much there; they were rather fond of bullying other kids, such as young Jobs. One day, he came home and declared that if he wasn't transferred to another school, he would stop going to school altogether. He was 11 at that time. Paul and Clara complied, and Jobs moved to the cozier city of Los Altos, so that he could go to Cupertino Junior High. This proved to be decisive factor for Jobs' future.

The location of the Los Altos home meant that Jobs would be able to attend Homestead High School in Silicon Valley. He began his first year there in late 1968 along with Fernandez was whom he had met there. Bill Fernandez, a neighbour who shared Jobs' interest in electronics. It was Fernandez who first introduced him to another computer whiz kid, an older guy named Stephen Wozniak, or as everybody used to call him, Woz. Jobs met Woz in 1969, when they were 14 and 19, respectively. At that time, Woz was building a little computer board with Fernandez that they called the Cream Soda Computer. Woz showed it to Jobs, who seemed quite interested in the idea. When Jobs arrived at Homestead High School, he enrolled in a popular electronics class. Woz and Jobs later engaged in several pranks together. It was also at Homestead that

Jobs met Chris-Ann Brennan, his first steady girlfriend, with whom he stayed for several years.

In the year 1971, Jobs finished high school. He decided to go to Reed College, a private Liberal Arts college in Oregon. However, the tuition fee at Reed was so high that Paul and Clara could hardly afford it. Nevertheless, they were bound by the promise they had made to their son's biological mother. So they spent almost their entire life's savings on their son's higher education.

Jobs officially stayed only for a couple of months at Reed. He dropped out before Christmas. However, this allowed him to 'drop in' on classes he was not supposed to attend.

It was at Reed that Jobs started experimenting with Eastern mysticism. He delved into weird books and came to believe that if he ate only fruits, for example, he would eliminate all mucus and not need to shower anymore. He also started fasting for long periods of time. One of his best friends at Reed was Dan Kottke, who shared his interests in such philosophies.

In the year 1974, Jobs desperately needed money; so he got a job at Atari. Atari was the first video game company which was created by Nolan Bushnell in 1972. Jobs looked up to Atari's founder Nolan Bushnell. He was impressed by this iconoclastic man who had made a fortune by building pinball machines. He was clearly an inspiration for Jobs to start Apple.

While he was still at Atari, Jobs asked his boss to fund a trip to India for him. Atari did pay his trip up to Germany, where he had to work on fixing some Atari machines. Thereafter, Jobs was joined by his friend from Reed, Dan Kottke, and they went to India in search for enlightenment. They came back, not enlightened, but with much experience.

The Beginning of Apple I

While Jobs was away in India his geek friend Woz was hired by Hewlett-Packard. To him, it was a dream job—a company full of passionate engineers, just like him, where he could work on products for other engineers. However, in his spare time, he had cultivated his interest in designing computer circuits, and had joined a computer hobbyists association called the Homebrew Computer Club.

Computers existed for a long time before Apple was founded. One of the first full-blown US computers ever built was ENIAC, in 1946. By the 1970s, the majority of large corporations were already equipped with computers. However, those were usually huge mainframes in giant computer rooms, built and maintained by industry mammoth IBM.

Personal computing was based on a radically different approach. It claimed that computers could be used by mere mortals, private individuals, instead of institutions. It was a revolutionary idea. It all started in 1974, when Mountain View based Intel introduced the world's first microprocessor—the 8080. All sorts of hobbyists started showing interest in how to use this powerful yet relatively cheap new piece of technology. A huge leap forward was made when a man named Ed Roberts launched the Altair, out of Albuberque, New Mexico. It was a computer kit based on the 8080, which people could assemble by themselves, a lot like the Heathkits that Jobs worked on in his childhood.

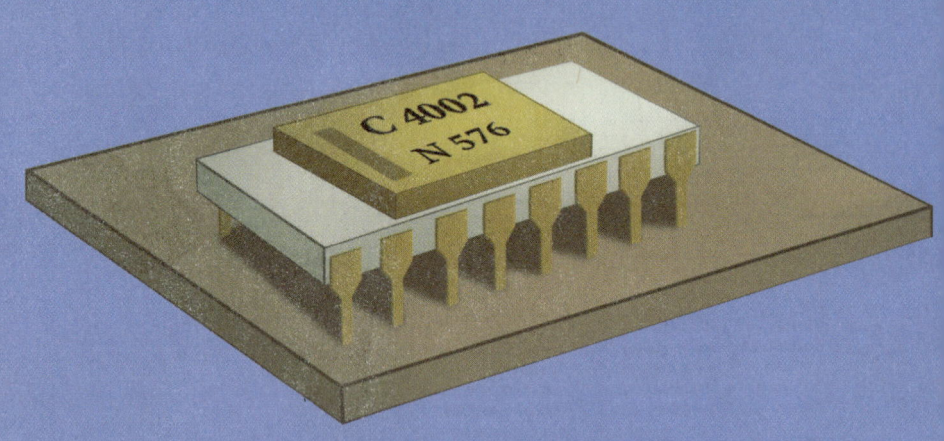

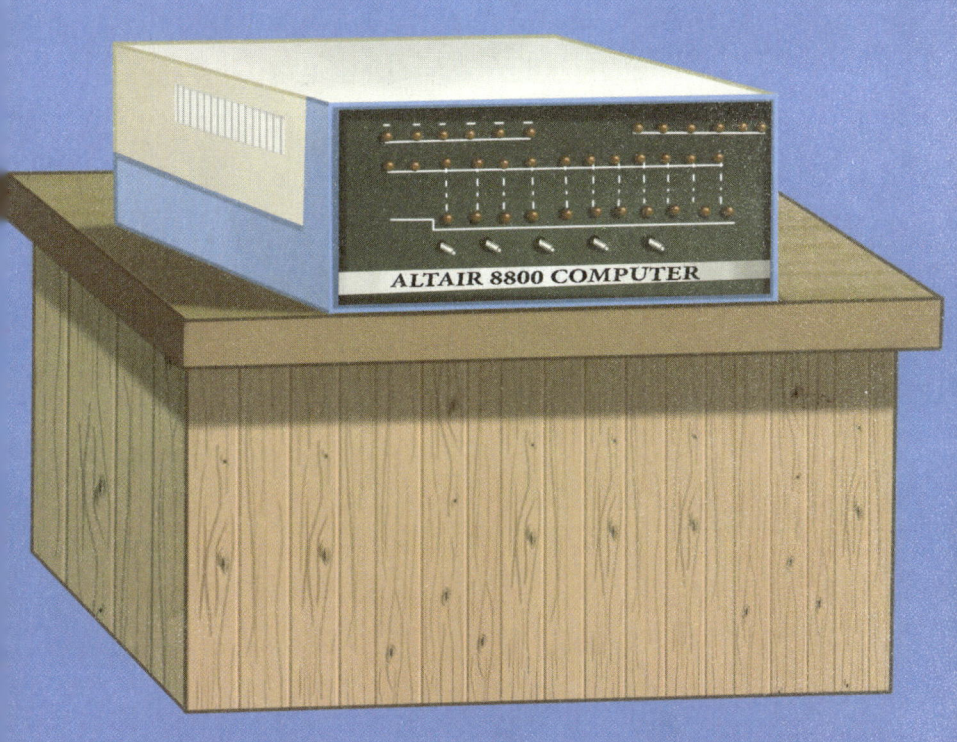

The Altair was basically a box that could flash lights on and off. It did not do much until Bill Gates and Paul Allen, who had just founded a new company called Microsoft, wrote a BASIC interpreter for it in 1975. The word spread around all over the country in those personal computing circles (which mostly consisted of engineers and radio amateurs). The Homebrew Computer Club, which operated from Stanford's Linear Accelerator Centre Auditorium, was one of those groups. Hobbyists would go there to show off their latest machine or programme they had worked on.

Woz was impressed by the Altair (and by Microsoft's BASIC interpreter), but he knew from his almost life-long experience in circuit design that he could do a much better job. So he started work on his own computer, which he decided to base on another microprocessor, MOS's Technology 502. This was his new goal in life. While keeping his job at HP, he worked very hard at this computer board, and came up with an impressive result—a powerful computer (for that time) which worked with a keyboard and screen, not one that flashed lights—and all that with amazingly few chips.

Woz showed his computer design to his friend Jobs, who was at once interested in the concept. Jobs did not

know much about engineering, but he could see there was a demand for having a computer to write software for, a computer for software hobbyists. He was especially excited to see that a lot of the qualified engineers at Homebrew were talking about Woz's computer with admiration. So he suggested selling it to them. He, along with Woz, would assemble the computers themselves and sell the whole board at Homebrew meetings.

To get the necessary US$ 1,000 to start building the first boards, Jobs sold his Volkswagen van, and Woz his HP

65 calculator. They thought about what to call the new company, but could not come up with a good name, until one day, Jobs said that they would call it 'Apple' if they did not find anything better. And so Apple computer was born!

One of Jobs' colleagues from Atari, Ronald Gerald Wayne, did the necessary paperwork to start a corporation and drew the company's first logo. As a result, he got 10 percent of the company's shares, while Jobs and Woz split the rest.

Apple computer received its first order from a Homebrew member called Paul Terrel. He was starting a new computer store called the Byte Shop, in Mountain View, and understood just like Jobs that there was a demand for such fully built computers. He ordered 50 of them, at US$ 500 a piece. That made the order worth US$ 25,000! It was a huge starting point for the young company, and got Jobs and Woz very excited. They started putting together the parts in the Jobs' garage, with help from his sister Patti and his friend from Reed, Dan Kottke. They paid them US$ 1 a board. The parts for the Apple cost US$ 220, while the computer was sold to Terrel for US$ 500, who would usually put it in wooden boxes.

This marked the start for Apple computers. Jobs and Woz had bought the other co-founder, Wayne, out for US$ 800, and incorporated the company on April 1, 1976.

Early Days of Apple

Woz started working on an improved design, the future Apple II, the very day he finished work on his first computer. Apple II was based on Apple I's design, but in many ways it was a huge breakthrough.

Firstly, it ran a lot faster with half as many chips. It also was the first computer that could produce colour! It could handle high-resolution graphics and sound, and had a BASIC interpreter built in. In simple words, it was the first computer that anybody who knew the BASIC programming language could use. It had all that it took to launch the personal computing revolution.

The prototype for Apple II was almost ready when Jobs and Woz took part in the Personal Computer Festival, held in Atlantic City in the summer of 1976. However, it was not ready enough to be shown to the public. Jobs and his friend Kottke were trying to sell Apple I from their Apple computer booth, while Woz was working on finishing Apple II. The visitors were not much impressed by Apple I, while MITS, which sold the Altair, had a huge booth with music, dancers and people in business suits. Jobs learned a valuable lesson that day.

After Apple II was finished, Jobs went looking for investors. He spoke with several venture capitalists in the Valley. Finally, Mike Markkula, a former Intel employee who had made millions and retired early, became the first investor at that time. He was 34 years of age when he met Woz and Jobs. He was also quite aware of the potential returns

on his investment. In Markkula's own words, "We're going to be a Fortune 500 company in two years. This is the start of an industry. It happens once a decade."

Markkula drew up a business plan. He wanted to invest US$ 250,000 to build 1,000 machines. This was a huge number by the young men's standards. Woz was also told

that for this to happen, he had to quit HP. At first he refused, since he was a huge admirer of HP and planned to work there his whole life. But Jobs pressed him hard into it, and eventually Woz gave in.

The new company got ready to show off their product at the West Coast Computer Faire, a conference held in San Francisco in April 1977. It was only a prototype, but the plastic case definitely made Apple II look like a professional product. Jobs negotiated a prime spot for Apple's booth, and took precious advice from both Markkula and Regis McKenna, the marketing guru of Silicon Valley. This is when Jobs bought his first suit for the occasion.

Apple computer received 300 orders for Apple II at the show alone, twice as much as the total number of Apple I ever sold! This was just the beginning.

In many ways, Apple II was both the start and the symbol of the personal computer revolution of the early 1980s. It was not only about Apple II's appealing design, its integrated keyboard, or its ability to plug into any TV to display colour graphics or play sounds; its built-in BASIC interpreter was also critical to its success, as it made the writing of compatible software very easy.

Only four years after it was started in a garage, the company was well on its way to fulfill Markkula's vision of belonging to the Fortune 500 elite of corporate America.

Preparing for the Future

Apple computer was growing at an incredibly fast rate. This was because there was no market for personal computers before! The company earned US$ 47 million in revenues in the financial year 1979, making Jobs a millionaire on paper. The company's board of directors, including its new members such as Arthur Rock and Don Valentine, began to discuss taking Apple public.

Meanwhile, the engineers in Cupertino started working on building Apple's future. Several projects came into being in those early years. In late 1978, there was Apple

III, which was supposed to build on Apple II's legacy. There was also a large re-organization at the top of the company. Apple III, which was introduced in the spring of 1980, had turned out a disaster in the marketplace. It was flawed and thousands of early models had to be returned to the company, whose only revenues still came from the sales of Apple II.

The next project, Lisa, became even more critical to the company's future. As a result, Apple computer was reorganized into three new departments—Accessories, Professional Office Systems (which included Lisa), and Personal Computer Systems (Apple II and Apple III). Jobs expected to head the POS division, but the board chose the milder and more experienced John Couch. Jobs was asked to chair the board instead.

The company started advertising in media, notably the *Wall Street Journal*, spreading the legend of the technical genius Steve Wozniak, and his friend, marketing genius and visionary Steve Jobs, who had started a revolution from their garage. There were full-page advertisements with pictures of Steve Jobs and Apple II, in which he was quoted as saying that the personal computer was a new kind of bicycle—a bicycle for the mind.

Jobs' personality was transformed during that period. He was increasingly recognized as a national icon, a symbol for the country's new entrepreneurial wave. He was starting to realize his dream of changing the world. Finally, on December 12, 1980, Apple went public. Even though the country was in the middle of a recession, the operation was a huge success beyond anyone's expectations. It was the biggest public offering in American history since the Ford Motor Company in 1956!

Macintosh

In 1983, while Jobs was in New York City, he met with Pepsi Co. executive John Sculley. Apple was still looking for a CEO, since the departure of Mike Scott. The board would not let 28-year-old Jobs run the company as he was way too inexperienced. Jobs lured Sculley into moving to California to become Apple's CEO and groom him into a full-blown manager. The words he used are now a legend in corporate history:

"Do you want to sell sugared water for the rest of your life or do you want to come with me and change the world?"

In Sculley's first months at Apple, his relationship with Jobs seemed almost like a honeymoon. Jobs considered Sculley a friend, taking him for his typical long walks on Stanford hills.

More importantly, Sculley agreed with Jobs' vision of making Macintosh the top priority at Apple. Throughout 1983, Lisa turned out to be unsuccessful in the marketplace, like Apple III before it. Apple was still relying only on its six-year-old Apple II computer, whose market share kept dipping because of the IBM PC. Macintosh had to succeed, or else the company would be out of business very quickly.

After Lisa came out in January 1983, the whole Lisa group joined Jobs and his team to get Macintosh ready for the market. However, nothing went smoothly. All the teams were late, and the management eventually had to decide on a date for the introduction of the product. They picked Apple's 1984 shareholders meeting, on January 24. There was also tremendous pressure to make software available to the new platform for the launch. Several software developers signed up, including market leader Lotus and Bill Gates' Microsoft, whose main business at the time was the IBM PC's operating system, DOS.

When the day finally came, Jobs once again proved his talent as a master showman. He introduced Macintosh as a revolution to a cheering crowd at Cupertino's Flint

Centre Auditorium. After what Apple had been through for the past three years, every hope turned to Jobs' Macintosh to salvage the company. Initially, the Mac did seem to be a huge hit. In the couple of months that followed its introduction, Jobs and the development team posed for countless photos, gave more than two hundred interviews, and ended up on several magazine covers.

But after this encouraging wave of early adopters, Mac sales started to drop. There were several concerns about Apple's computer. First, it was painfully slow; it was also a bit pricey, selling for US$ 2,500, a thousand more than the IBM PC it was supposed to compete with. But the biggest drawback was its software. Macintosh being a brand new platform, almost no programme could run on it when it was launched, whereas a tonne of applications were already available on the IBM PC platform. Everyone agreed that Macintosh was a lot friendlier and easier-to-use, that its technology was far superior to that of the IBM PC; but it was useless.

Steve Quits Apple

There was increasing resentment building up against Jobs at Apple. The two men—Sculley and Jobs—increasingly criticized one another in their inner circles. Even Woz, who felt deeply insulted by the treatment the Apple II team received, left the company in February 1985.

For Jobs, it became a personal war with Sculley. In the year 1985, Scullley confronted Jobs in front of the other Apple executives. After hours of intense discussions, they simply could not find a solution to the conflict between the two men. Jobs said he would take a vacation until they were done with the re-organization, and left. It was only a few days later, on May 28, that Sculley informed him that the board had decided on a new organization chart, which did not include Jobs at any managerial position.

Jobs' conviction that the board would support him had proved wrong. He lost the final battle.

During those four months, from May to September 1985, Jobs continued to chair the board. He was not fired from Apple, contrary to popular belief. But he had a lot of time on his hands, and tried hard to find out what he was going to do next.

At that time, Jobs was still looking for new directions in life when he met a friend of his, Nobel laureate Paul Berg, from Stanford University. Berg told him of his work on DNA, and asked him whether the molecules could be simulated on computers. The answer was no, not yet anyway. This gave Jobs the idea of starting a new company. He would build a high-end computer aimed solely at the higher education and research markets.

As he was still at Apple, he decided to inform the board of his decision. On September 13, 1985, he described his plan. The board seemed enthusiastic at first, even willing to invest in the chairman's new venture. But when Jobs announced who would join him in his new company, called NeXT, they turned bitter. He went away with Bud Tribble, the first Mac programmer; George Crow, a key Mac hardware engineer; Rich Page, who had supervised almost all of Lisa's development; and a few other key people from Apple. Apple felt threatened, especially since they were themselves working on a 3M machine code-named Big Mac. On September 17, Jobs announced his resignation from Apple to an assembly of stunned journalists who had gathered at his mansion in Woodside.

Beginning of NeXT

NeXT did not have an easy start. The moment it was created, the six co-founders were sued by their former employer, Apple.

Apple was accusing them of stealing their technology. As a result, in its first year or so of existence, the new company could not work on any product in particular,

since there was a chance they would lose the trial and would have to give all the technologies they had worked upon back to Apple.

In the meantime, Jobs set up to build a perfect company.

He started by doing one of the things he was best at doing—recruiting. He hired only extremely bright and competent people. It seemed like the whole Valley wanted to work at NeXT. Among its first employees was Avie Tevanian, a software genius who was still a student at

Carnegie Mellon University when Jobs met him. He was working on a UNIX kernel called Mach. Jobs told him that if he joined NeXT, his invention would run on millions of computers in a few years' time.

NeXT treated its employees in a unique fashion. First, there were only two levels in salary for a long time: the senior staff earned US$ 75,000 a year and the rest earned US$ 50,000. It gave the place sort of an interesting feel, comprising a community of super-bright people, not a tech start-up driven by greed. Other perks included health

club memberships, counselling services, emergency loans, and free fresh juice. The company still had no revenues to speak of during those early years. It was still operating with Jobs' own money!

A critical change occurred when, in November 1986, CBS aired a documentary called The Entrepreneurs, which featured Jobs during NeXT company retreats. One of the viewers was a millionaire Ross Perot, who had become immensely rich by selling his company Electronic Data

Systems to General Motors. So captivated was he by the documentary that he immediately phoned Jobs and said, "If you ever need an investor, call me."

It was good news as NeXT was burning money at an incredibly fast rate. So the deal was quickly signed in February 1987. They announced Perot's investment of US$ 20 million in exchange for 16 percent of NeXT, while Jobs kept 63 percent for himself. The company had no product but a T-shirt back then and yet it was already valued over US$ 125 million! This is how powerful Jobs' name was in the mid-1980s. Perot joined the board of directors together with Carnegie Mellon administrator Pat Crecine, a good friend of Jobs.

Personal Life

Steve Jobs' personal life had several crucial evolutions. First, after years of research, he had finally found his biological family. His biological mother Joanne was still alive, and she had actually married his father a couple of years after Steve was born. They had given birth to a daughter, Steve's biological sister, named Mona.

Mona Simpson was a young yet accomplished writer who had just published a novel, *Anywhere But Here*, which had earned her several literary prizes. Jobs was thrilled that his sister was an artist! He filled a bookshelf at NeXT with free copies of Mona's book.

Jobs also started to fully accept his 9-year-old daughter Lisa as family whom he had denied even fathering. She increasingly spent time at his home in Woodside, and he even took her to NeXT's offices every now and then. He even started to get deeply involved in her education.

Gradually, he became more stable in his relationships and started thinking of marrying his girlfriend, Tina Redse.

This whole period in Jobs' life is documented in the book *A Regular Guy*, a novel by Mona Simpson which barely disguises Jobs and Lisa as its main characters.

The years from 1991 to 1994 were the worst in Jobs' career. Ironically, they were also some of the happiest years in his private life. In 1990, at the age of 35, after his girlfriend Tina Redse had turned down his proposal, he started dating a young Stanford MBA student named Laurene Powell. Laurene was extremely smart and independent. The two got married on March 18, 1991, in Yosemite. Jobs only brought along a couple of guests in the lodge's chapel, and the simple ceremony was conducted by his long-time Zen guru Kobun Chino. A few months later, Laurene gave birth to Jobs' second child, a baby boy named Reed Paul, after Jobs' alma mater (Reed College) and his father (Paul Jobs).

Jobs Returns to Apple

Jobs' leaving and then coming back to Apple forms a rich part of Apple's history. To understand how Jobs came back to the company he founded, it is necessary to have a look at Apple's situation in the mid-1990s.

Apple made healthy profits from 1986 to 1995. Everyone who wanted a user-friendly computer bought a Macintosh for approximately US$ 2,000, half of which were pure profits.

However, at the beginning of 1992, Apple felt threatened by an emerging super power in the computer business, Microsoft. So far Microsoft was mostly known for providing MS-DOS to the IBM PC and its clones, which accounted for somewhere around 80 percent of the PC market—the remaining 20 percent being Apple. But the Redmond-based company was also an application developer, and it

had actually worked on the Macintosh with Jobs in the early 1980s to provide Mac software, such as Multiplan.

When Bill Gates saw the GUI of the Macintosh in 1982, he also understood that this was the way of the future, a future which threatened his DOS franchise. So he started working on a Microsoft GUI that could be added on top of MS-DOS: Windows. For years, Windows was so terrible that nobody in the industry took it seriously. However, Apple started feeling threatened when it became better and more Mac-like, especially after the release of Windows 3.0 in 1990. As early as 1988, Apple sued Microsoft for stealing 'the look and feel' of its Mac operating system. The case ended in court in 1994, and Apple lost. The following year, in 1995, Microsoft launched Windows 95, which was the most successful GUI release in the history of personal computing. Almost every PC user upgraded and started using GUI, while Apple lost its monopoly.

The sales of Macintosh started going down dramatically. The company was losing market share, and getting rid of its successive CEOs did not seem to help. The company was going downhill, failing to deliver new products on time and lagging behind in software development.

The first talks of Jobs going back to Apple started in 1995, even before Gil Amelio was appointed CEO. In December of that year, Jobs' friend Larry Ellison, the founder and CEO of Oracle and one of the world's richest men, talked about making a hostile takeover bid for Apple in the media and on his website. All the arrangements were made for Oracle and other investors to purchase the company for about US$ 3 billion and install Jobs as its new boss.

It was one year later that Jobs' return to Apple was set into motion. In November 1996, the company was looking for a new operating system for its future Macs. The Mac OS was replete with old technologies, slow and unadapted to modern computers. Apple had been working for some time on an internal project called Copland, yet it was constantly being delayed and it soon became obvious it would not fit the bill. So, CEO Gil Amelio started shopping around for a modern OS to buy. And after a while, people at Apple began to think on Jean-Louis Gassée's software BeOS, which had everything Apple needed, including the good taste of running natively on Apple's products. Gassée was the former Apple France executive who was supposed to replace Jobs as the head of the Macintosh division in 1985. He had since left Apple and started his own company.

However, some NeXT employees called up Apple and told them about their own system, the very advanced NEXT STEP that had always been regarded as one of the best software platforms on the planet. When Jobs learned about it, he was taken by surprise. However, in December 1996, he showed up at Apple for the first time in 11 years and not only convinced the board of using his technology, but also to buy his company. Apple agreed to pay more than US$ 400 million for NeXT, which was much more than what others had offered.

Jobs also agreed to take the stage at Macworld Expo in January 1997. The show painfully showed how disastrous the company's management had become under Amelio, with sales that fell 30 percent below their 1995 level. The situation did not improve in 1997 and the company lost US$ 700 million, making the total losses under Amelio amount to over US$ 1 billion.

It had become unbearable for Apple. In July, the board of directors, led by Jobs' ally Ed Woolard Jr., ousted Amelio after 500 days on the job, and asked Jobs to become the company's new chairman and CEO. He declined, accepting only to become a member of the board and an interim CEO, to supposedly help the company get back on track before handing over the position to somebody else. He was concerned about being CEO of two public companies at the same time—Pixar and Apple. After he came to power, he reformed the board to install his friends. The new members were all supporters of Jobs.

After this incident, Jobs used all his energies to put Apple back on track. He surveyed every single product team in the company, calling them in one by one in Apple's conference room. Everybody had to convince him that their product was essential to the company's strategy. There was no sentimentality. If the product was not making a profit, it had to go. He soaked up a tremendous amount of information about all aspects of the business before taking action. After two years as interim CEO, Jobs completely turned Apple around. He restored the company's public image, implemented a successful and focused new strategy, attracted software developers, and launched highly innovative and awe-inspiring products in the marketplace. Apple regained its old-time glory.

The End of a Super Inventor

In October 2003, while performing a routine abdominal scan, doctors discovered a tumour growing in Jobs' pancreas. He was suffering from an islet cell neuroendocrine tumour. It is a kind of tumour that can be removed by surgery but it usually leaves the patient with hardly 10 more years of life.

But Jobs being under the spell of Eastern mysticism of his youth and his strange yet deep beliefs about medicine and food, stubbornly refused to undergo the surgery, sticking to a special diet that he thought would cure him of his cancer! This madness lasted for nine long months, while his family and Apple's top people got increasingly concerned about him. However, observing that his situation was not improving, he reluctantly agreed to have the surgery done in August 2004, at the Stanford Medical Centre. It was only then that the news was made public, with Jobs himself writing a letter to Apple employees from his hospital bed. He took a month off and came back as CEO in September, assuring everyone he was cured. This first event was felt as a shock by the Apple community worldwide, but it was even more shocking to the company's shareholders, who argued that they should have been aware of the CEO's diagnosis much earlier considering his importance to the company.

Also, it was later revealed that Jobs underwent a liver transplant in April 2009. The transplant worked, and Jobs went back to Apple in late June 2009, as planned.

A few years went by with Jobs functioning normally. Finally, on October 5, 2011, Apple Inc. announced the demise of its co-founder. After battling pancreatic cancer for nearly a decade, Jobs died in Palo Alto. He was 56 years old at that time.

The later innovations of Apple included revolutionary products as the Macbook Air, iPod and iPhone, all of which have dictated the evolution of modern technology. Apple carries on with the dream and vision of Steve Jobs, gifting us all with wondrous products from time to time.

Timeline

- **1955** Steve Jobs is born on February 24, in San Francisco to Abdulfattah Jandali and Joanne Simpson

- **1955** He is adopted from infancy by Paul and Clara Jobs in San Francisco; moves to Mountain View, California, five months later

- **1969** He is offered a summer job at Hewlett-Packard Co. (HP) by William Hewlett

- **1971** Jobs meets Steve Wozniak, his partner with whom he later founded Apple Computer Inc.

- **1972** Jobs graduates from Homestead High School in Los Altos

- **1972** He registers at Reed College, Portland, Oregon, and drops out after one semester

- **1974** He joins Atari Inc. as a technician

- **1975** He starts attending meetings of the Homebrew Computer Club, which discussed home computers

- **1976** Jobs begins Apple Computer Company with Wozniak and Ronald Wayne

- 1976 Jobs and Wozniak launch Apple I for US$ 666.66, the first single-board computer with a video interface and an onboard Read Only Memory (ROM)
- 1977 Apple launches Apple II, the world's first widely used personal computer
- 1979 Development of Macintosh starts
- 1980 Apple III is launched
- 1980 Apple goes public, share price jumps from US$ 22 to US$ 29 on the first day of trading
- 1981 Jobs involves himself in Macintosh development
- 1983 He recruits John Sculley as Apple president and CEO
- 1983 He announces Lisa, the first mouse-controlled computer but it fails in the marketplace
- 1984 Apple launches Macintosh with a splashy ad campaign
- 1985 Jobs is ousted from Apple after boardroom struggle with Sculley; Jobs resigns and takes five Apple employees with him

Timeline

- **1985** He founds Next Inc. to develop computer hardware and software; the company is later renamed Next Computer Inc.

- **1991** He marries Laurene Powell; bears three children with her

- **1992** NeXT releases NEXTSTEP operating system for Intel Corp. 486 processors; it fails in the wake of competition from Microsoft Corp.'s Windows and IBM Corp.'s OS/2

- **1997** Jobs becomes interim CEO and chairman of Apple Computer Inc., after Amelio is ousted

- **1998** Apple releases the all-in-one iMac computer, which sells millions of units, financially reviving the company and boosting its share price by 400 percent; iMac wins the Gold Award from British Design and Art Direction

- **1998** Apple returns to profitability and records four profitable quarters in a row

- **2004** Jobs is diagnosed with pancreatic cancer and undergoes surgery; recovers and returns to work in September

- **2007** Jobs announces the iPhone, one of the first smartphones without a keyboard, at Macworld Expo

- **2009** In early January, Jobs says that his dramatic weight loss is caused by a hormone imbalance; around one week later, he says that he will take a leave of absence from Apple until June due to his medical condition; the Wall Street Journal reports that Jobs underwent a liver transplant; Apple confirms that Jobs is returning to work at the end of the month

- **2010** Apple announces the iPad tablet computer, which becomes an instant success

- **2011** Apple announces Jobs is taking a medical leave of absence, without specifying a reason for the leave or how long he would be away; later that year, Jobs announces that he is stepping aside as CEO, with Cook taking over that role

- **2011** Jobs dies on October 5

Activities

Assignment

Find out the story behind the logo of Apple.

Research Work

Here is a list of Apple products. Research them on internet and write a detailed report on how these products have revolutionized the world.

iPod

Apple Watch

iPhone

iPad

MacBook

Questions

1. What is Steve Jobs known for?
2. When and where was he born?
3. Who were his biological parents?
4. Describe the nature of Jobs as a child.
5. How did Jobs meet Steve Wozniak?
6. What was the common interest that they shared that later became the cause of their success?
7. Which company is known to be the first manufacturer of video games?
8. Who was its founder?
9. A sum of US$ 1,000 was needed to build the first computer board. How did Jobs and Woz gather the money?
10. In what ways was Apple II better than Apple I?
11. Who was Mike Markkula?
12. In West Coast Computer Faire, a conference was held in San Francisco in April 1977. What was the response for Apple II?

Activities

13. Who was John Sculley?

14. Although Mackintosh seemed to be a hit, it had serious flaws. What were they?

15. Why did Jobs establish NeXT?

16. What were the facilities given to the employees of NeXT?

17. Who was Mona Simpson?

18. Whom did Jobs marry?

19. What was the relation between Microsoft and Apple?

20. What were the medical reasons for Jobs' untimely death?

21. Make a list of some of the Apple products.

Glossary

acknowledged: something that is recognized as being good or important

amateurs: a person who is a beginner in an activity

auditorium: the part of a theatre or concert hall

bullying: to use strength or influence to harm or scare someone

complied: to act in accordance with a wish or command

decisive: to settle an issue

decline: to diminish in strength or quality

diagnosis: the identification of the nature of an illness

disappointed: to be sad or displeased

disaster: a sudden accident

disastrous: something that causes great damage

electronics: the branch of physics dealing with the design of circuits

eliminate: to completely remove or get rid of

enlightenment: the action of enlightening

enrolled: to officially register as a member of an institution

enthusiastic: having intense and eager enjoyment

expensive: something that costs a lot of money

Glossary

iconoclastic: attacking cherished beliefs or institutions

innovative: introducing new ideas which are original and creative

inspiration: being mentally stimulated to do or feel something

interim: a provisional period or arrangement

mass media: the diversified media technologies that are intended to reach a large audience

microprocessor: an integrated circuit that contains all the functions of a central processing unit in computers

negotiate: to bring about an agreement by discussion

prankster: a person who is always playing pranks

prowess: expertise in a particular activity

recruiting: the procedure of enlisting someone in the armed forces

salvage: to retrieve or preserve something

shareholder: one who owns shares in a company

stubbornly: being determined not to change one's attitude or position on something

transplant: to move or transfer someone or something to another place

tremendous: great in amount or intensity